£1.75

D1439054

THE LEAVES OF SOUTHWELL

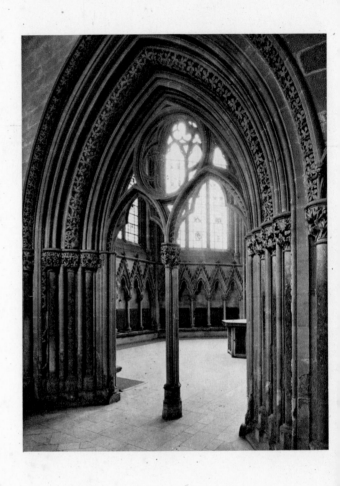

Chapter House Portal

THE
LEAVES OF SOUTHWELL

by
NIKOLAUS PEVSNER

Lecturer in the History of Art, Birkbeck College,
University of London

Photographs by
F. L. ATTENBOROUGH

Principal, University College, Leicester

The KING PENGUIN *Books*
LONDON *and* NEW YORK
1945

THE KING PENGUIN BOOKS

Editor : N. B. L. Pevsner
Technical Editor : R. B. Fishenden

MADE IN GREAT BRITAIN

Printed by
HARRISON & SONS LTD.
44-47 St. Martin's Lane, W.C. 2
Set in Monotype Perpetua

PUBLISHED BY

PENGUIN BOOKS LIMITED
HARMONDSWORTH MIDDLESEX
ENGLAND

PENGUIN BOOKS INC.
245 FIFTH AVENUE
NEW YORK

Be Thou praised, O Lord, for all Thy creation,
More especially for our Brother the Sun,
Who bringeth forth the day and giveth light thereby,
For he is glorious and splendid in his radiance,
And to Thee, Most High, he bears similitude.

Be Thou praised, O Lord, for our Sister the Moon and the Stars,
In the Heavens Thou hast set them bright and sparkling and beautiful.

Be Thou praised, O Lord, for our Brother the Wind,
For the air and for the clouds, for serene and for tempestuous days,
For through these dost Thou sustain all living things.

Be Thou praised, O Lord, for our Sister the Water,
For she giveth boundless service, and is lovely, precious and pure.

Be Thou praised, O Lord, for our Brother the Fire,
Through whom Thou givest light in the night hours,
For he is beautiful and joyous, vigorous and strong.

Be Thou praised, O Lord, for our Sister, Mother Earth,
Who doth nourish us and ruleth over us,
And bringeth forth divers fruit and bright flowers and herbs.

From St. Francis's Hymn of the Sun [1]

Fronde nemus induitur
Iam canit philomela,
Cum variis coloribus
Iam prata sunt amena,
Spatiari dulce est
Per loca nemorosa;
Dulcius est carpere
Iam lilium cum rosa,
Dulcissimum est ludere
Cum virgine formosa.

From the Carmina Burana [2]

THE LEAVES OF SOUTHWELL

*To Major L.W., C.M.F., to remind him of
the good things on our side of the Alps*

The leaves of Southwell to which this little book is devoted are the leaves which adorn the capitals of the columns of Southwell Chapter House. The Minster of Southwell lies eight miles west of Newark and fourteen miles northeast of Nottingham. Southwell Manor was given by King Eadwig to the Archbishop of York in 956. The church is mentioned early in the eleventh century as collegiate—that is, forming part of a foundation of secular canons. York, Ripon, and Beverley are the other mediæval collegiate churches in the province of York. The Chapter of Southwell was dissolved under William IV; in 1884 the church was raised to cathedral rank. Its current name, Southwell Minster, would point to a monastic establishment. But the Cathedral of York and the Collegiate Church of Beverley are also known as minsters. The building consists of a Norman nave and Early English choir, the chapter house, and a rood-screen and sedilia of about 1330.

Figure 1   Entrance Arch between Choir and Passage to
                                        Chapter House

The chapter house was erected to the north of the choir. The two parts are connected by a passage with a modern wooden roof. Between choir and passage is a portal divided by a central shaft into two arched openings (fig. 1). The passage was originally open towards the east—in cloister fashion. Its north end is a higher vaulted rectangular ante-room from which, turning east, we reach by another double archway (frontispiece) the polygonal, free-standing chapter house. Passage and chapter house seem to have been designed and carried out at the same time.

No records have survived which would enable us to date the two chambers exactly. But it is known that in 1293, John de Romaine, Archbishop of York, gave instructions that certain fines raised from canons who would not repair their houses within one year should be applied " ad fabricam novi capituli."[3]

Polygonal chapter houses are an English speciality.[4] The earliest of which we know are attached to Lincoln Cathedral and Beverley Minster. A few are decagonal; Southwell, York and most of the others are octagonal. Only in Southwell and York have the master masons been so bold as to dispense with a central shaft to support the far-stretching ribs of the vault. However, when it came to constructing the vaults, the York mason lost his courage and chose timber instead of stone. Southwell alone has a stone vault without a prop in the middle. The feat is less, it must be admitted, than it would have been at York ; for Southwell Chapter House measures only about thirty feet across, York about sixty. Salisbury and Westminster (with central shafts) have diameters of about fifty to fifty-five feet. It is characteristic of the English chapter houses to be lit by generously spaced windows, nearly filling the walls above the seats for the chapter on all sides except those where the entrances are. Below the window zone at Southwell there are thirty-six seats. They are separated by slender columns, supporting pointed trefoiled blank arches. Above the arches are steep gables resting on heads or foliated corbels. Foliated tympana fill the spaces between arches and gables. The gables carry crockets and reach with their finials just into the zone of the windows (figs. 4 and 5). These have simple geometrical tracery, trefoils and quatrefoils in circles, as against the somewhat more complicated forms of the other contemporary chapter houses. The windows give lightness and airiness to the room, deepened and enriched originally by the glow of stained glass. Salisbury, Westminster, or Wells, with their central shafts, may afford more variety of vistas. York, without a central shaft, adds spatial interest by chapter seats, each in its own little polygonal niche surrounded by five dark miniature columns (fig. 17). Southwell holds no surprises of this kind. Any spatial complications are avoided. Structure and decoration are of the same Mansfield limestone. Southwell's pride is its unbroken width saved from baldness by a beauty of foliage decoration unparalleled in thirteenth-century chapter houses. You find the leaves of Southwell, fresh and resilient, lustily spreading all over the capitals of the forty-five columns which separate the seats, all over the tympana, crockets and finials of the gables above the seats, all over the vaulting shafts and bosses of the roof, all over the capitals and voussoirs of the double archway leading from the chapter house into the passage, and that from the passage into the choir, and all over the capitals of the forty-nine little columns along the west side of the passage and its originally open east side.

The abundance of foliage at Southwell is only

matched at York, and there—in accordance with the undulating palisade of small columns—the capitals are much smaller. The wall rhythm of York Chapter House is quick and lively, that of Southwell a noble and vigorous stride, youthful, yet stately. It is worth while to stress this difference between the two structurally related chapter houses. For in the style of their foliage they belong closely together. The sculptors of both York and Southwell challenge the conventions of Early English—that is, Early Gothic—leaf decoration, and go for inspiration to nature, the nature, it seems, of the English countryside. They are not the only artists who experienced this change of heart, nor are they the earliest, though perhaps the earliest in England, but the similarity of their work remains striking.

Looking at the comfortably wide entrance arch which connects Southwell choir with the passage to the chapter house (fig. 1), or at the arcades of the passage (figs. 2 and 3), the magnificent archway between passage and chapter house (frontispiece), or, finally, the interior of the chapter house itself, the impression of the foliage in general is of live, manifold form and strong contrast of dark and light; in detail it is one of amazing truth to life. Capitals had been the favourite place for foliage ornament in Norman days. But then the scrolls and leaves used were but a surface decoration of the block-shaped capitals, undercut perhaps, but never so deeply as to destroy the solidity of the basic blocks. Now the nobly moulded capitals, with their bell shape, as it appears unadorned in the choir arcades of Southwell, are almost hidden—though not quite hidden—behind a filigree of scalloped leaf. In the later centuries of the Middle Ages the foliage becomes crowded and tends to smother the structural form behind. Southwell keeps a happy balance between ground and pattern.

Figure 2   *West Wall of Passage between Choir and Chapter House*

East Arcade of Passage between Choir and Chapter House

Figure 3

This balance, the key-note of all that is great in the chapter house and, as will be shown, in the thirteenth century, was consciously achieved by the master of Southwell. Proof are the leaves spreading above the chapter house capitals and partly covering up the springing of the trefoiled pointed arches (Plates 7, 8, 11, 15, 17, 18, 21, etc.). Leaves on capitals, whether as luxuriant as those of the Greek and Roman Corinthian and composite orders or as hieratic as those of Norman and pre-Norman days, have a functional justification. The capital is a halt, a junction, and, therefore, provides leisure for looking at ornament. But a leaf right at the springing of an arch has no such *raison d'être*. It must be the caprice of an artist who knew very clearly how far he could go in veiling functional lines without confusing them. This conceit of structure seen through openwork occurs also in the voussoirs of the outer and inner archways (figs. 2 and 3, Plates 1 to 3). Here the effect is one of delightful ambiguity, with the leafage rounded out so as to form a convex moulding all along the arch and the concavity of the true moulding just discernible behind. Again, the same effect is obtained in the jambs of the two archways—and there it is most piquant of all (figs. 2 and 3, Plates 2 and 3). The outer archway has one column each side, the inner three. In neither case do the columns reach close to the actual openings of the doorways. There, in a structurally sensible way, the mouldings appear undisguised. However, just because this is so obviously sensible, the artist is not satisfied with it. He will have his fun. He must show his mastery by breaking rules, or at least questioning them. So on each side of each archway just one spray of leaves bends over at capital height into the reserved zone of the inner door jamb.

Balance of structure and decoration—a precarious,

14

Figure 4   *Stalls 7, 8 and 9 with Capitals C.9 to 12*

Figure 5

Stalls 32 to 36 with Capitals C. 38 to 45

Figure 6

Tympana of Stalls 7 and 8

adventurous, proudly and self-consciously sustained balance—is one of the achievements of the Southwell capitals. Another is balance between nature and style. The copying of nature, for reasons ranging from primitive magic to sheer pride in imitative skill, is amongst the earliest functions of art. So is the desire to create expressive or decorative pattern out of material from nature.

At Southwell a degree of truth to life is reached which never between the first and the thirteenth century had been attempted in the West. Yet nowhere is the result that plodding, painful, pedantic pettiness of detail which spoils so much academic flower drawing and flower modelling of the nineteenth century. What saves the Southwell masters from this pitfall is their faith in the integrity of pattern. Look at Plates 7, 8, 15 and 22, to choose a few of the most accomplished. They reveal how carefully the coherence of the pattern has been preserved in spite of the sway and scalloping of the leaves. Stone must remain stone and not attempt to masquerade as vegetable matter. However, the sculptor has nowhere gone so far as to force his leaves into decorative symmetry. Leaf, he felt, must remain leaf and never be reduced to abstract pattern. He respected his material—stone — precisely as much as his subject—leaves. This is how he could achieve unity, while at the same time preserving variety; and this is how he could avoid tediousness, while confining himself to a far smaller number of botanical genera than the casual observer would realise.

As for the botanical side of the Southwell capitals, this has been studied specially by the late Professor A. C. Seward.[5] The plan on the facing page and the numbering of the capitals adopted in this book are taken from his paper on Southwell. His identification of the

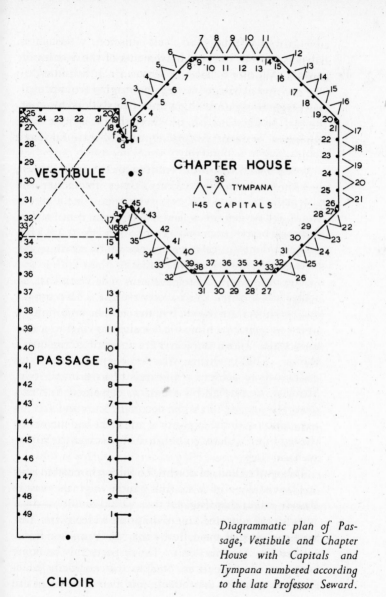

Diagrammatic plan of Passage, Vestibule and Chapter House with Capitals and Tympana numbered according to the late Professor Seward.

different plants has also been adopted, although in certain cases he wavered between two or three possible genera. In other cases Professor E. J. Salisbury, to whom I was privileged to show photographs of the capitals, suggested yet other genera. I have added his comments, marked (E.J.S.), where he disagrees with Professor Seward. According to Professor Seward's tables, maple is found thirty times in capitals, spandrels and roof bosses, oak twenty-six (or twenty-eight) times, hawthorn nineteen (or twenty) times, ranunculus and potentilla nineteen (or twenty) times, vine eighteen times, ivy twelve times, and hop eight (or nine) times. Rose and bryony each occurs twice ; and there are a few odd and doubtful cases of fig, geranium, wormwood, bittersweet, cherry and blackthorn.

The impression the non-botanist receives is that the artist had a quick eye to observe the characteristic features of certain leaves, but no scientific ambition. It never occurred to him, for instance, to keep to a uniform scale. Hawthorn leaves are no smaller than maple leaves. This confirms what has been said about his endeavour to achieve a synthesis of nature and style. The leaf, despite all his accuracy, remained to him a decorative motif. It is the decorator's joy and skill, in association with the explorer's, and in the end mastering the explorer's, that accomplish the miracle of the Southwell carvings.

This quality can, of course, be fully appreciated only in front of the originals. And if these originals were in France rather than England they would doubtless draw numbers of educated English pilgrims to see them. Yet, being so close at hand, few know of them, and fewer still have really seen them. The plates to this book are meant to whet appetites. Sculpture is essentially three-dimensional. No reproduction in two dimensions can do it justice. But Mr. Attenborough's photographs of the Southwell capitals are an almost perfect interpretation. They have as much depth as the camera can achieve without smudging detail to obtain dramatic contrasts. Moreover, photographs have two advantages over originals which are not universally recognised or at least admitted. They focus the reader's attention on important detail that he might miss on the actual spot, drawn from capital to capital by their multiple interest. And, as they lie on a table or are reproduced on the pages of a book, they can be enjoyed and studied with more comfort and leisure.

So now—before any more general questions are asked—the plates must speak for themselves, and little will be needed by way of comment.

Passing through the archway from the choir, you reach the passage and on your right the arcades which formerly opened on to the small yard (fig. 3). The columns are short and slim, and have capitals only one leaf high (Plates 4 and 5). The leaves extend along the cross lintels towards the outer capitals that once faced the open yard. Plate 4 (V.4 in Professor Seward's numbering) is oak, needless to say, with sharply modelled acorns, and Plate 5 (V.5) hawthorn in happily spaced sprays.

Directly you have reached the dividing line between the passage and the taller rectangular ante-room the scale and magnificence of the capitals grow. You are near the climax of the approach now, the archway into the chapter house (frontispiece). So the foliage of the capitals is now two leaves high (Plate 1). The capitals (V.17 and 16) have buttercup on the right, just left of the shaft which divides the corridor from the ante-room, thorn on the left, with vine leaves and grapes up along the outer moulding of the archway.

The flatness of the vine leaves makes a beautiful contrast with the dark shadows betraying the hollow moulding. The leaves are not symmetrically arranged, but in just regular enough an alternation to convey the impression of conscious pattern. The scale of the leaves also is similar enough to allow vine, thorn and buttercup all to share in the same play of ornamental form.

Plates 2 and 3 take us to the archway itself, the most splendid *ensemble* that the master composed. It corresponds in the thrill of expectation which it is meant to create to the west façade of the French cathedral with its array of figures of saints. So here is the greatest luxury of foliage, here alone an alternation of light and dark stone, here the most consummate mastery of carving, a treatment occasionally almost too free to keep within the bounds of structural decoration. Yet the leaves veiling the deep mouldings below and above the capitals have again that exquisite crispness and un-erring rightness of placing which we have seen before. Two dragons play amid the foliage, small and innocuous looking creatures. These artists were no longer as obsessed by monsters as their elders a hundred years before. There are few animals altogether at Southwell, and they are nowhere very conspicuous. It is a human-ised and strangely civilised nature that the genius of the carver evokes.

The species represented are from left to right : Vine along the moulding, hawthorn (Plate 30), maple (with ranunculus flowers, or, as Professor Salisbury suggests, ranunculus leaves and flowers, Plate 12), maple in the moulding above; and ranunculus (Plate 17) in the capital next to the doorway; and then, on the other side, still from left to right, ranunculus (E. J. S. : potentilla ; Plate 16), vine (E. J. S. : a lobed-leaved form of mulberry ; Plate 6), with maple in the moulding above, and oak

(Plate 10), with vine down the right-hand moulding. All these genera and those of the other capitals belong to the English countryside or garden. Vine, it must be remembered, was also not alien to mediæval England. It could be grown to-day, too, and drunk enjoyably, provided it was treated, as our forebears did, with honey and water.

The sculptors might have chosen many more genera, beech leaves, elm leaves, willow, aspen, honeysuckle, convolvulus. No doubt, one reason why they did not was that they apparently realised the higher decorative possibilities of deeply dissected leaves as against simple ovals or pointed ovals. Another reason may have been that they wanted to keep to a fairly uniform type of leaf.

This reason helps perhaps to explain the curious fact mentioned before that the hawthorn leaves of Southwell appear as large as the maple or vine leaves. But this disregard of scale has a deeper cause. The thirteenth century had no ability or wish yet to place individual objects into relation with each other or nature as a whole. It is the same in the figure sculpture of French cathedrals. Beyond a relation of two figures—say, the Virgin and Elizabeth in the Visitation, or Abraham and Melchisedek—no sculptor was able to go. Thirteenth-century sculpture is pre-Euripidean. The stage reached is that of Sophocles—that is, of classicity.

But it is Western, not Greek classicity. Hence, the eager effort towards specific likenesses which is so alien to the Periclean Age. Look at the vine (E. J. S. : mulberry ?) of capital *b* (Plate 6). The carving is as sharp as if the stone were wax. The bunches of grapes, on the other hand (if they are grapes), are summarily treated, neither characteristic in general shape nor in texture It has been said before how wittily the artist places odd leaves over structurally critical joints. Here again the

23

one vine leaf on the right stretches out from the capital to cover the shaft separating the two columns with their capitals and abaci.

The same hand must have carved the vine (E. J. S. : mulberry ?) of capital C.36 (Plate 7). The treatment of both foliage and grapes is identical. Much is broken off at the foot ; fortunately, it has not been restored. In York Chapter House enjoyment is badly impaired by so much painstaking and pedantic restoration. The composition here, and in capital C.11 (Plate 8) is a simple alternation of upward and downward leaves, with grapes to fill the intervals. Yet C.11 cannot be the handiwork of the same artist, even if his design. The execution seems a little wilder and less precise, with the bunches of grapes stylised differently. That more than one carver was at work is proved beyond doubt by capital C.20 (Plate 9) with its coarser technique and smaller scale. The composition here reads clearly in two horizontal strips. Less attention is paid to the individual leaf. On the other hand, the carver of C.20 had a feeling for atmosphere which the other carver could not have tolerated, because it would have blurred the brittle *finesse* of his technique. It is well in keeping to have here and only here a bird among the grapes, picking at them in the dark shadow at the foot of the capital. The texture of the feathers comes out excellently, but avian accuracy was hardly aimed at.

In the representation of oak, the same two attitudes occur. Capital *a* (Plate 10) immediately right of Plate 6 is sharply modelled and intertwined in the grouping, capital C.12 (Plate 11) has the two-layer arrangement, and a general undulating movement.[6] Detail is weaker, but an atmospheric unity of foreground form and background shadow is approaching. In this more telling treatment of space the fourteenth century seems nearer, and perhaps one can even distinguish some of its approaching nobbliness of foliage. Two examples from Southwell of this approaching style will be illustrated later (figs. 8 and 22).

Yet another instance of the two chief Southwell attitudes towards foliage: the maple (E. J. S.: ranunculus repens) of capital *e* (Plate 12) and capital C.39 (Plate 13). The differences are exactly the same as described before. The separation of the two layers of the foliage is especially evident in Plate 13. No less evident is the close interest of this (younger?) artist in depth of space. The master of the entrance arch sees leaf besides leaf, each a perfect specimen. The other reads front to back as well as left to right.

But there are still more individualities distinguishable. The plant on the abacus above capital C.19 (Plate 14) is of a kind which one would not expect to find so close to the nature-inspired capitals of the chapter house. It belongs, with its springy leaves coiling over into bud-like

lobes, to that somewhat more conventional type of foliage which characterises the Early English style of about 1200 — 1260. There is even a complete capital in the same style (C.17, fig. 7). It looks strangely incongruous between the realistic maple leaves on the left and the realistic ivy leaves on the right. Evidently, then, some older member of the team still worked on in the style of his youth,

Figure 7   *Capital C.17*

25

Figure 8   Boss of the Chapter House Vault

while the younger master mason and all his other assistants had already turned to another more complicated
style.

But taking the chapter house as a whole, we cannot
even say that the style of the master mason, that is, the
style of the archway from ante-room to chapter house, is
the end of the development. To look at the bosses of
the star vault (fig. 8) is to see already revealed the
arrival of that flowing and flickering style of the early
fourteenth century known as Undulating. Botanical
correctness is no longer so important. A new unifying,
less personal tendency is at work. Had the master
mason changed, or had he chosen to leave a free hand
to one of his younger assistants ? We do not know.

What follows from the presence of early thirteenth
century and early fourteenth century looking foliage in
the chapter house is that the great art of our leaves belongs to a short moment only in the development of
mediæval carving. Hardly thirty years this summit was
held. The tomb of Archbishop Walter de Gray in York,
who died in 1255, is still in the Early English conventional style, while the majority of capitals of the nave of
York, which was begun in 1291, tends already towards
the Undulating or Decorated style.

What also follows from the three different styles in
the same room is that the individual craftsman must
have had a considerable amount of personal liberty.
We know from many documents that one of the principal jobs of the master mason was to draw templates
of mouldings then to be applied mechanically to the
stone by routine workers. But it comes as a surprise
to us, used to building methods of the twentieth century, to see that capitals were permitted so entirely
out of keeping with the chief designer's taste as those
with conventional foliage must have been. In this

connection it may be worth a word in passing that capital C.5 (Plate 15) has miniature diamond friezes in the top and bottom mouldings, while the neighbouring capitals have nothing of the kind, though again capitals C.14 and 15 (Plates 23 and 24) have. C.5 incidentally shows the winged fruit of maple with the leaves—a rare if not unique speciality of this particular carver. Still, while individual differences of selection and treatment are interesting enough, their importance should not be over-emphasized in thirteenth-century work. For they never endanger the decorative unity of the whole as they do in Renaissance and post-Renaissance decoration.

Of flowers, the buttercup is most often and most exactly portrayed. Capital c (Plate 16) is part of the archway into the chapter house. The horizontal along the jamb, therefore, dominates over the vertical (see Plate 3). This the artist has felt and indulges in a luxuriant spread which would hardly be called for in the capitals of the isolated columns inside the chapter house, such as C.13 (Plate 17), and still less in the magnificent capital of the centre shaft of the archway (Plate 18). Here a very tall capital crowns a slender and much spliced shaft and supports light and transparent tracery. So the master, with great sensitivity, has confined his work to two rows of clearly separated ranunculus leaves with generous bare spaces below the lower and below the upper row. Where on the sides of the archway he had the same depth of capital to play with, but no reason to stress slim erectness, he introduces an additional row of leaves which connect these two rows into a richer pattern (Capital d, Plate 19). Where, on the other hand, he has less height of capital and yet the wish to convey dense growth, he finds two rows sufficient, but telescopes them slightly (Capital

Figure 9   Hop-Decoration of Arch-Springings above Capital C.41

C.4, Plate 20). Capital C.4 has the flowers badly damaged. Capital *d* (Plate 19), however, seems never to have had flowers. The young leaves appear a little clumsy in the photograph. This is due to the unhewn stone being visible behind them. From below, where the onlooker usually stands, they recede into the dark background.

They are somewhat similar to the faithfully portrayed female fruit of the hop on Capitals C.34, 10, and 14 (Plates 21 to 23). The composition of Plates 21 and 22 is reversed, but otherwise all but identical. This is the first indication of what will be discussed in more detail later, namely, that the carvers did not go direct to nature but used drawings or patterns, in this case probably the same. There is sufficient evidence all over Europe to prove that master masons spent their *Wanderjahre* working in the lodges of other countries or other parts of their own country, and then set up on their own with a stock of drawings from work studied.

Plate 21 emphasises the ribbing of the leaves, Plate 22, by the master of the archway, prefers the smoother surfaces. Plate 23 was built up on the same scheme as the other two—leaf behind leaf fanwise opened up with the fruit in between—but by an adherent of the dynamic school, or perhaps " the dynamic master." The diamond friezes have been mentioned before. They, too, add movement. The stems of the plant along the foot of the capital are characteristically twisted.

In his treatment of bryony (Capital C.15, Plate 24) the same artist has created the same effects. Again the stems are twisted, again the diamond friezes carry on the restlessness of the carving into the zones of the mouldings, and again the whole appears dramatically *mouvementé* : wind-swept, as it were. Capital C.42

(Plate 25) seems static and a little dull in comparison. Maybe the loss of half the bottom leaves destroys what might otherwise have been a satisfactory balance. The carving itself is as good as any in the chapter house.

As a supreme dramatic effort, the "dynamic master" introduces into one Capital (C.24, Plates 26 and 27) a scene of struggle, two hounds attacking a hare. Ivy surrounds the scene and conveys the right atmosphere of undergrowth. But there, once more, the century's realism ends. There is no consistency of scale between leaves and beasts, nor is there much sense in the use of this particular plant to accompany this particular scene. Moreover, the three animals are very summarily carved and in their relative positions wholly converted into pattern. The leaves grow as they do in nature ; the hare and hounds are rendered in an odd bird's-eye view, although those who examine the capitals would never look down on the scene. It is the same lack of feeling for nature as an all-embracing medium that we noticed before. The observation and accurate rendering of true three-dimensionality became only possible with the dawn of the Renaissance. It is no accident that linear perspective was discovered early in the fifteenth century in Italy and the unity of landscape concurrently by the illuminators of Flanders. Our thirteenth century conquered the shapes and texture of individual objects—which was indeed a memorable conquest—but it did not venture into their relations.

However, to account for the mask-like lifelessness of the head above Capital C.31 (Plate 28) this explanation will not suffice. The thorn leaves and flowers of the capital are treated as knowledgeably as any. And sculptors in France and Germany between 1235 and the end of the century carved heads no less life-like and

31

telling than this foliage. Rheims and Naumburg are there to attest it. In England no figure sculpture exists equally true to nature. This may be due to chance destruction ; certainly the dissolution of the monasteries and the Civil War did much to rob the country of its former treasures. Else it may be due to the fact that English sculptors were never at their best rendering the human form in three dimensions. The statues of Wells do not promise the quality of Rheims amongst the lost cycles. Britain has not given birth to any imager as great as the architect of Lincoln, the decorator (in the absence of a better name) of Southwell, the illuminators of the Gorleston and of Queen Mary's Psalters, or John Constable. On the other hand, it may be argued that the head at Southwell is treated as a mask, with sprays of hawthorn sprouting from the forehead and from beneath the chin, quite similar to ornamental heads in Villard de Honnecourt's text-book (see below) and at Rheims, and, therefore, had to be stylised. However, this argument does not really hold good. For above other capitals, C.22 for instance (Plate 29), and as corbels to support most of the gables, there are heads, too, and these heads are nearly as far removed from the throbbing life of the foliage below. So it seems to remain true that, for whatever reason, realism in physiognomical observation did not keep pace in England with botanical realism.

The thorn leaves of Capital C.22 are especially agitated, and the leaves of hemp nettle shooting up between the thicket of hawthorn[7], although again seen in a bird's-eye view, help to create that feeling of a wilderness, of many things growing closely together and seen together, which remained, as a rule, beyond the conception of the thirteenth-century artist.

In Capital f (Plate 30) the hawthorn has berries,

not flowers. The capital belongs to the richest kind. The way in which the lower row of leaves curves forward to form a cup is exceptional, and very successful. The transition from the three-dimensional treatment of the thorn in the capital to the much flatter treatment of the vine along the upright hollow on the left is also exemplary. The sculptor of the hawthorn (E. J. S. : buttercup) capital on the west of the outer archway (Plate 31), that from choir to passage, was too keen in his sense of life in nature to accomplish such subtle balance. In his eagerness to carry on with his zigzag of leaf, he filled his upright hollow with a mass of flickering foliage, where his calmer and wiser brother chose individual vine leaves to spread them as a smooth openwork cover for the dark moulding behind.

Plate 32 (Capital C.9) is, because of its ruinous state, a good example to show the technique by which these openwork effects were obtained. The masons probably cut a cone to cover the whole of what was to be mouldings and foliage. They then set to work chiselling out leaves and flowers and scooping out behind them until the mass was reduced to top and foot mouldings and a rough cylinder behind the filigree of natural form. Whether this was done "avant la pose" or "après la pose"—that is, while the blocks were still in the workshop or after they had been placed in position—cannot be said.

Plate 32 is of interest botanically, too. The rose leaves (or are they potentilla ?—E. J. S.) are as fresh as any of the others, but the flowers are—one cannot help thinking—consciously stylised. In looking at them association connects them more readily with the Tudor rose of heraldry than with the roses we see in gardens. Why is that so ? Professor Seward says : " I have never seen a wild rose with more than five petals, but as the number of flowers examined is comparatively small, it would be rash to assert that doubling does not occur in the wild state. In cultivated roses . . . the occurrence of two series of petals is not uncommon. The rose was the badge of Elinor of Provence, Queen of Henry III . . . A golden rose was the badge of Edward I . . . . It would be worth while to trace in more detail the history of the cultivated rose, but this . . . must be left for the present. The main point is that the Southwell flowers are probably copies from a cultivated and not from a native wild rose.'' While this states the main botanical problem, it does not offer an explanation of the psychological puzzle. Why does just one kind of flower appear not true to nature, but wholly as a pattern. The possible solution may be that for the rose the West had already established a heraldic convention so firmly that an artist would adhere to it unconsciously instead of looking afresh at roses in gardens and along hedgerows, or at drawings from work done in front of actual specimens. That roses were grown in monastic and princely gardens we know from many sources [8]. As early as about 800 Charlemagne's *Capitulare de Villis* has lily and rose, together with such herbs as sage, rue, rosemary and many others, in a list of plants to be grown on royal demesnes. A generation later the ideal plan for a monastery which a clerical member of Louis the Pious's Court sent to the Abbot of St. Gaul contains beds for very much the same herbs, while the only flowers provided for are again lily and rose. One of the earliest mentions of roses in England must be the passage in which we are told of William Rufus forcing his way into Romsey Abbey, where the future Queen Matilda was educated. The Abbess hid the child, and William, trying to find her, stepped into the cloister as though he "only wanted to admire the roses and other flowering plants." A rosebush said to be of the same period still exists in the cloister of Hildesheim Cathedral in Germany. Poets of the twelfth and thirteenth centuries also sing of no flowers more fondly than of lily and rose, and encyclopaedias of the same period (see below) describe roses fairly regularly. An early English encyclopaedia, Alexander of Neckham's (died 1217) *De Natura Rerum*, suggests explicitly that gardens should be adorned with "roses and lilies, heliotrope, violets and mandrake," besides sage, mint, coriander and other herbs.

So artists, we may be sure, were familiar with the shape of the rose, and if they did not portray the flower as they saw it, they must have had a strong reason. The one suggested here may be as good as any.

But if we talk of the artists or even of the sculptors of Southwell, what do we really mean? Was there such a thing as an artist, as a sculptor in the thirteenth century? In other words, can the characteristics which make the modern artist, the artist of the centuries since the Renaissance, be at all credited to the Middle Ages? How far are social status, professional approach, and even creative impulses comparable then and now? An answer to these questions is bound to be somewhat involved. But it must be attempted all the same, because without it we would remain in the dark about the personality—can we say, the genius?—behind the leaves of Southwell, and personality and genius are what have interested the West for the last hundred and fifty years more than all else in the contemplation of works of art. Who, then, and what, to repeat our question in a more personal form, was the master who some 650 years ago took such a keen pleasure in the countryside, had such intimate knowledge of trees and flowers, and such consummate power to render in stone their freshness, softness and resilience?

His name is not recorded. But then, surprisingly few names of artists and architects of the Middle Ages have come down to us. They are not mentioned by the chronicles, because their work was but regarded as competent craft. Neither the term architect nor the term sculptor was in use. Architecture and sculpture issued anonymously from the cathedral or abbey lodge, that is workshop, not because there was no creative genius, but because it was taken for granted. If we hear of master masons of cathedrals or of sculptors, it is usually only by chance records of wages paid or by chance deeds.

It is not even strictly right to speak of sculptors. As far as can be made out, the building and the decoration of a mediæval church were done by a team or gang assembling wherever there was work. It was led by a master mason versed in both architecture and sculpture and, when the work was completed, either broke up or migrated to another job. Master masons may, of course, have chosen their men so that a figure specialist and a foliage specialist were amongst them, but there is no evidence in corroboration. On the contrary, a few cases exist which point to the master mason's evenly balanced interest in both building and carving.

At Bamberg Cathedral in Germany the west towers are evidently derived from Laon in France [9]. The mason must have studied the towers there and brought home drawings as inspiration in his future work. Though these were modified considerably in the Bamberg towers, they are copied more correctly in little canopies above some figures of masterly carving inside the church. These figures, amongst the finest of their century, are evidently free paraphrases of sculpture at Rheims. Rheims is not far from Laon. So we have to imagine the young carver working and learning in Northern France and then, later, assuming charge of the Bamberg lodge to design both building and decoration.

The National Library in Paris possesses a thirteenth-century manuscript that proves the unity of architect and sculptor as well as the freedom of travel and study during the time to which we owe Southwell. Villard de Honnecourt [10] wrote and drew this book as a text-book for the youngsters of his lodge. He addresses them and promises to give them "grands conseils de la grande force de maçonnerie, et des engines de charpenterie, de la force de portraiture (that is, of the art of drawing) comme l'art de géométrie." And he tells them more than once, in a manner more personal than anything the history of art possesses of so early a date, where he saw the things he drew, what impressed him, and what he recommends for imitation. And so we learn that he came from the north of France, looked round and drew at Rheims (aisle windows of the cathedral, "because I liked them best") and Chartres, and even went as far from home as Lausanne and Hungary. And we also see him—evidently in charge of a lodge—placing on record roof constructions and ground plans as well as figure sculpture—a seated Christ, a Deposition, a Mount of Olives, Ecclesia and Synagogue, a Crucifixus—and the foliage of a bench end, and also wrestlers, men on horseback, a falcon, and lions, explicitly called "copied from life."

Such a man the master of Southwell must have been. The wide, airy chapter house interior has the same freshness and serenity as the foliage of the capitals. Whether the designing architect carved them himself or how many he carved himself we cannot say. He certainly did not do everything with his own hands. It would have been materially impossible. Also it has been shown that at least two distinct major personalities can be traced in the carving of the capitals. In spite of this, however, the design of the chapter house and its decoration are homogeneous, and that—whatever the nineteenth century may have said in praise of original handwriting—is what really matters.

Now, the next question is the designer's nationality. Was he an Englishman? That is by no means certain. For we must remember that Villard the Frenchman went to Hungary to work there. It is also recorded in one of the most interesting of mediæval building histories that the architect of Canterbury Cathedral choir, William of Sens, came from France specially to get the job as master mason to the cathedral. And the east parts of Westminster Abbey are so evidently influenced by Rheims, that the name of the first master mason, Henry de Reyns, may very well be an anglicised form of Henry of Rheims. The master of Bamberg, on the other hand, can by comparison of his handwriting with that of local predecessors be proved—as nearly as arguments of style can prove anything—to have been a German with French experience.

It is necessary to mention these two possibilities, because the realism of Southwell is not an individual innovation in the sense in which, say, Masaccio's and Uccello's perspective was about 1420 and Picasso's and Braque's cubism about 1908. The master of Southwell had obviously studied in detail one of the central works of Gothic architecture and decoration in Europe : Rheims Cathedral. Here—and also, incidentally, in the Sainte Chapelle in Paris—we can still see capitals strikingly like those of Southwell, capitals with oak,

Figures 10 to 13   Four Capitals from the Triforium Gallery
of Rheims Cathedral

Figure 14   Inner Wall of West Front, Rheims Cathedral.
St. John the Baptist reproaches Herod and Herodias.
With leaf panels above and below.

buttercup and many other leaves on the same scale as at Southwell. They are to be found on the triforium gallery of the nave (figs. 10, 11, 12, and 13), also, though in a rather more summary treatment, on the friezes above the heads of the figures of the west portals, and, most exquisitely, but a little later, above and below the rows of figures on the inside wall of the west front (fig. 14). The chronology of the work on Rheims Cathedral is intricate, but indications point to dates about 1230–1240 for the west portals, about 1250–1260 for the triforium gallery and about 1275–1285 for the decoration of the west wall.[11] The Sainte Chapelle was built from 1243 to 1248. It can safely be assumed that the master of Southwell knew France and especially Rheims.

There is, in point of fact, a very similar case at Naumburg Cathedral in Germany. Here, about 1255–1265, capitals were carved which are of the very

Figure 15   *Buttercup Capitals from the Rood Screen,*
Naumburg Cathedral

41

Figure 16　　　*Vine (or Passion flower ?) Capitals from the Rood Screen, Naumburg Cathedral*

same family, again with vine, hawthorn and other native leaves (figs. 15 and 16). Again, connections with Rheims are confirmed by the figure sculpture ; and again, just as at Bamberg, these figures have so strong a local flavour that a French sculptor can be ruled out.

So the question must now be asked for Southwell Chapter House whether it is, as we see it, the creation of a Frenchman working in England or of an Englishman familiar with France. There are no figures at Southwell to help a decision. But there is another line of reasoning even more conclusive than arguments of sculptural style.

Southwell belongs to the province of York. The only other polygonal chapter house without a central pier is that of York. Its dates are not more precisely known than those of Southwell. The nave at York was begun in 1291. Its foliage decoration is very much like that of Southwell, but just a trifle more stylised—not in the early thirteenth century way of the Southwell choir, but towards the new undulating style of the fourteenth century. The capitals of the chapter house, however, have (or had before their devastating nineteenth-century restoration) the same observation of nature and the same fondness for native plants as those of Southwell (figs. 17 to 20). The only dates we have regarding York Chapter House are those for the stained-glass windows and their coats of arms. They make it likely that the chapter house was structurally complete by 1307[12]. The choir of Southwell, too, mid-thirteenth-century work, as has been said before, is clearly of York (an earlier York) style. So it can be safely assumed that the Southwell mason was an Englishman, grown up in the tradition of York, a man of greater sculptural genius than the decorator of York. All the same, it is highly probable that he had direct knowledge of Rheims. There is nothing unlikely in that, since France, and especially what was growing up rapidly of cathedrals and churches in and around Paris, was the international centre of Gothic art.

Moreover, to confirm the English connections of the Southwell master, the cloister of Lincoln, dated approximately 1296, has leaf capitals of the same style and perhaps school (fig. 21), simpler than the best work at Southwell, but extremely similar to that of the miniature cloister east of the Southwell passage (Plates 4 and 5). Lincoln had been the chief Eastern rallying point of progressive English architecture from the end of the twelfth till after the middle of the thirteenth-century. But with the completion of the Angel Choir, about 1280, its leadership came to an end and passed to York. The exquisite flower of English early fourteenth-century decoration was, it seems, rather of Yorkshire than of East Anglian origin, although the beauty of work in this

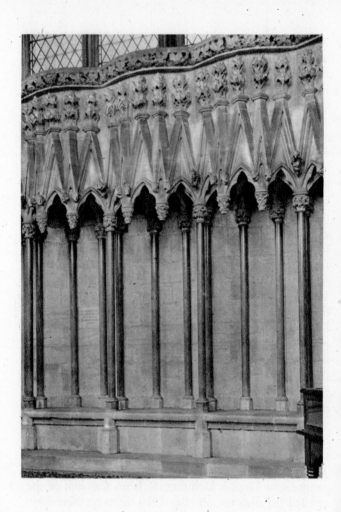

Figure 17   Three Stalls from York Chapter House

Figure 18   Detail from one of the Canopies of
                                                    York Chapter House

Figures 19 and 20   Details from Canopies of
                                      York Chapter House

style in Lincolnshire and at Ely is just as fascinating as at
Beverley, Selby, and at Southwell itself, where about
1325 a rood screen was built to separate the choir
from the western parts. This has a central entrance
and seats under canopies on the choir side. Behind
one of them, the first to the south of the entrance,
the wall is decorated with a diaper pattern of exquisite
quality (fig. 22). So the foliage of Lincoln must be
regarded as an offspring of the York-Southwell style,
although the case of Naumburg has clearly shown that
independent conversion to the realism of Rheims
occurred in widely separated parts of Europe.

One of the few examples inside England of such in-
dependently rising foliage realism is the leaf decoration
of St. Frideswide's shrine at Oxford (figs. 23 and 24),
not so accomplished as Southwell and probably a little
earlier. Its historical context is not yet sufficiently

Figure 21   *Vine Capitals from the Cloisters of*
Lincoln Cathedral

Figure 22   *Panels from the back of one of the Stalls,*
Southwell Minster

Figures 2 3 and 24   *Leaves from St. Frideswide's Shrine,*
Oxford Cathedral

known. It may point to London and the King's masons. However, that is outside the scope of our investigation. All that matters here is to show that other workshops besides that of York knew of the French innovation and accepted it.

Thus the conception which forces itself on one's mind is that of English (as well as German and, incidentally, Italian) masons wandering to France, learning at Rheims and the other contemporary cathedrals and churches, and returning with their sketch-books full of notes of what they had seen and helped in. In these sketch-books they had careful drawings of realistic French capitals, which they reproduced when they came back. In their architectural style they resumed the traditions of Early English, but their foliage remained French, though details like the nettle of Plate 29 prove that they checked their drawings by going direct to nature and that they enjoyed themselves thoroughly in doing so. This phase of French influence, however, was short. Soon their successors shook off the foreign harness and created that indigenously English version of mature Gothic, the Decorated, which, with its undulating decoration and its delightful ogee arches, remained a strictly national achievement until in its turn it began to influence France.

The moral of this story is that travelling and study abroad were more frequent in the Middle Ages than we assume, and that not everything that looks like a direct copy from nature need be the result of drawing from life. Paris, the Ile de France and the Champagne are the places where the masons were introduced to this new attitude to nature, as they were the centres of æsthetic and intellectual life altogether.

The greatest of the thirteenth century scholastics, that is the philosophers, theologians and scientists—for there was no distinction between the three yet—all at some stage studied or taught at the University of Paris : the Franciscans Alexander of Hales (an Englishman), St. Bonaventura (an Italian), and Roger Bacon (another Englishman), as well as the Dominicans St. Thomas Aquinas (another Italian) and Albertus Magnus (a German).

Franciscans and Dominicans are the two characteristic religious orders of the thirteenth century. Founded in 1209 and 1215 they introduced into monastic life the new spirit of awareness to everyday life with which this book is concerned. They preferred the bustle of the towns to the rural solitude of the Cluniac and Cistercian monasteries. Cloistered peace had favoured the other-worldly meditations of earlier monks. Franciscans and Dominicans chose to mix with burgess and tradesman. As the monks of the eleventh and twelfth centuries had formed the clerical counterpart of the self-contained manorial life on the secular side, so the friars, exponents of a worldlier age, correspond in their choice of abode and activities to the life of the mediæval town with its guilds. The urban mind is more agile than the countryman's, more self-confident and less inclined to take authority and tradition at their face value. The townsman's senses react more quickly and his tongue is keener to communicate what his eyes have observed.

Thus we find about the time of the Rheims capitals the Franciscan Salimbene's fresh and vivid narrative of current events in Italy. We find—if we look for examples of this new world-openness in other fields and other countries—the direct, conversational style of the stories in Robert Mannyng's *Handlynge Synne*, and the daring Latin poetry of the Wandering Scholars, amorous, bibulous and always out for the pleasure of the moment. An exquisite example forms one of the two mottoes to this volume. We find the hard-hitting satire of Reynard the Fox, and the troubadour's deification of his fair lady, and his delight in wood, flower and bird-song. Of this, just one early example in the original Provençal, a poem by Bernard of Ventadour :

> " Quan l'erba fresque e'l fuelha par,
> E·l flor botona el verjan,
> E·l rossinhols autet e clar
> Leun sa votz e mou son chan,
> Joy ai de luy, e joy ai de la flor ;
> Joy ai de me, e de mi dons major.''[13]

(When green herbs and leaves appear, and flowers bud in the green grass, and the nightingale raises her voice, high and clear, and sings her songs, I have great joy in her, and joy in the flowers, joy in myself, and still more in my lady.)

Proofs of this new worldliness appear everywhere, in the Sweet New Style of Italian poetry (developed under Provençal influence), the praise of chivalrous virtues in the French and German romances, the fullness of new experience in Marco Polo's accounts of his journey to the Far East, and in the strange blend of western learning with Arab and Spanish traditions of science and magic in the mind of Frederick the Second. He had been brought up in Norman Sicily and regarded Sicily as the centre of his Empire. But at the same time he built castles and palaces in Southern Italy in a French Gothic style with French architects, and the gate of Capua in a revived Roman style. This rediscovery of antique art which culminated in the work of Niccolò Pisano, the most famous of mediæval Italian sculptors, and a contemporary of the later sculptors of Rheims, is also noticeable in a few of the best pieces of figure sculpture at Rheims Cathedral itself, notably the Visitation of the west façade.

It need hardly be emphasized that the same new understanding of Antiquity helped Western philosophy and science to overcome some of the prejudices of the early Middle Ages[14]. Here again a spontaneously increasing receptivity and a growing knowledge of Aristotle's system, transmitted first through Arabic translations, and later the Greek originals, led to opposition against the accepted faith in authority and to a new faith in experiment or rather experience. Roger Bacon's " Oportet omnia certificari per viam experientiae " is the most frequently quoted statement. But Bacon said hardly more than William of Auvergne, Bishop of Paris from 1228 to 1249, had said before him in his De Universo, and Bartholomew the Englishman in his De Proprietatibus Rerum of about 1230-1240. William's De Universo is directed against those who lightly choose recourse to God and miracle to explain incidents on this earth without first seeking for natural reasons. This attitude makes William more sceptical against the superstitions of his age than most of his contemporaries. He does not deny occult forces—nobody did at that time—but he knows that what appears magic may be illusion and what appears demons may be vapours. A particularly telling example of this thirteenth-century insistence on experience is Bartholomew the Englishman's comment on the well-known story of the beaver which was supposed to castrate itself to escape the hunter. The story comes from one of those punning etymologies typical of the Middle Ages : The Latin for beaver is *castor*. Hence *castrare* and the tale. But Bartholomew, whose book incidentally contains a good deal of entertaining observation of daily life, adds drily that the untruth of the story can be proved any day by looking at beavers which one may find (" quotidie patet in castoribus qui inveniuntur ").

The most interesting example, however, of this new curiosity—and this leads right back into the problem of Southwell—is that of Albertus Magnus (*c.* 1200-1280), the most learned and most prolific writer of his century. His faith as a Christian and a theologian was in no way impaired by his research into nature. But his confidence in his own senses made it—sometimes, if not always—possible for him to restore a balance between science and revelation or between experience and authority such as Europe had not known since the days of Aristotle. The following passage is significant enough : " It is not sufficient to know in terms of universals (what he means is : in a general way) ; we must seek to know every individual thing according to its own nature. For this is the best and the most perfect kind of knowing."[15] However, while William of Auvergne and certainly Roger Bacon might have said that too, neither was capable of anything like the precision with which Albert in his *De Animalibus* and *De Vegetabilibus* (comments on translations of Aristotelian or pseudo-Aristotelian treatises) describes animals and plants.[16] He knew that he was doing something there that had not been done before and apologises for it. At the beginning of the twenty-second book of the *De Animalibus* he says that the alphabetical method of listing animals which he proposes to use may "not be appropriate to philosophy," but that it appears better suited "to instruct rustic minds." And again, he begins his sixth book *De Vegetabilibus* by saying : "In this book we satisfy the curiosity of our students rather than philosophy ; for philosophy cannot deal with particulars."

So Albertus Magnus did not offer his inductive method as a substitute for the accepted methods of scholastic philosophy—his *De Vegetabilibus* starts, in fact, in the usual way, with a whole book on the soul of the plant and the meaning of life in a plant. This he simply takes over from his source, Nicholas of Damascus, the author of the treatise which Albertus believed to be by Aristotle. But when it comes to the parts which we should call scientific, then Albertus abandons Nicholas's text and writes them entirely afresh, in the form of digressions, as he calls them.

Now the digressions of the sixth book, *De Speciebus Quarumdam Plantarum*, with its subdivision into alphabetical lists of trees and of herbs (including flowers), have, it will be proved, an important if indirect bearing on the Southwell capitals.

To understand their significance, they must be seen against the background of botanical description before Albertus. There existed in the Middle Ages two kinds of books in which flowers and trees were discussed : the plant-books proper, usually illustrated, and the encyclopædias. Of the plant books proper, Professor Charles Singer, in a detailed study published some twenty years ago [17], showed how the accuracy of pictorial representation declined from the exquisite quality of the colour drawings in the sixth-century Vienna manuscript of Dioscorides's Herbal to the stylised symbols of plant types—often so similar to Norman capitals—in eleventh and twelfth century manuscripts.

As for the encyclopædias and the treatises which Albert would have called philosophical, no such survey has yet been made. The following is no more than a sample to tempt some botanist or horticulturist into more thorough research. The sample consists of passages about maple and oak, the two trees most frequently occurring at Southwell. They are taken from six authors, ranging from St. Isidore of Seville, who wrote in the seventh century, to Albertus Magnus. The others are St. Hildegarde of Bingen (1098-1179), the abbess and visionary, Bartholomew the English-man, a Franciscan, whose *De Proprietatibus Rerum* has been mentioned before and apparently dates from about 1230-1240, Thomas of Cantimpré, a Flemish Dominican, whose exactly contemporary *De Natura Rerum* has never yet been printed in full, and Vincent of Beauvais, whose *Speculum Naturae* of about 1250, is part of one of the longest and most comprehensive of all mediæval encyclopædias. It deals, as also do the *De Natura Rerum* and the *De Proprietatibus Rerum*, with the whole macrocosm and microcosm : the universe, God, angels, man, his soul and body, animals, plants, stones, metals, and so on.

The maple, by all these writers save one, is confused

with the plane, that is, appears as *Platanus*. Now here is what Isidore, in his *Etymologies,* the most popular of pre-thirteenth-century encyclopædias, says of *Platanus* : " *Platanus,* so called after the width of its leaves, or because the tree itself is broad and wide. For πλάτος is the Greek word for wide. The name and shape of this tree is mentioned in the Bible, where it says : ' Like a plane tree, I am spreading this way and that by the water in the streets.' It has very tender and soft leaves, similar to those of the vine. "[18] This is the only sentence which Isidore devotes to description.

St. Hildegarde does hardly more. As she often prefers vernacular to Latin names of plants, she calls her chapter on the maple [19] rightly *De Ahorn,* the German word for maple. She then starts with the Aristotelian statement about the specific element and humour of the tree. The maple is, she says, cold and dry, " and whoever has fevers of short or long duration should boil the twigs of this tree with the leaves in water, and if he frequently takes baths in this water, and as soon as he leaves the bath, crushes the bark, presses out its juice, pours it into pure wine, and drinks it cold after the aforesaid bath, and does this often, his fever will cease and his troubles vanish. And if somebody is suffering from ' gicht ' (the German word for gout) in one of his limbs, he should take of the timber of the same tree, heat it by the fire and then put it hot on the place which hurts, and the ' gicht ' will go. Or if he cannot bear the timber in its solid state, then he should powder some of the hot timber, put it on the place which hurts, and fix it with bandages, and he will feel better. But if somebody's nose is swollen . . ." And so it goes on with superstitious prescriptions and without a word to tell us what the maple looks like.[20]

When it comes to Bartholomew, some seventy-five years later, a period very near to that of Rheims, this is his disappointing comment on the maple : " Platanus is a tree so called from the width of its leaves, because they are broad and wide. For the Greeks called wide *planus,* as Isidore says, 51, 17. Its beauty is mentioned in the Bible, which says : ' I am exalted as a plane tree,' Ecclesiasticus 14.[21]   It has soft and tender leaves, similar to the vine leaf, as Dioscorides says ". To this he adds that the plane tree is cold and dry, and that its leaves are useful against complaints of a hot and moist nature. " For, it is said, they will heal rheumatism and inflamed swellings of the eyes (sties ?). A decoction of the bark and leaves suppresses toothaches, and, it is said, pains in other bones, too. It is supposed to have the virtue of mitigating acute pains. It is also supposed to be good against burns, if applied with other palliatives. A decoction in wine is also said to be of value against poisons. This tree is praised by Pliny, book 12, chapter 3."[22]

Thomas of Cantimpré is, if anything, worse—that is still less original : " Platanus is a tree so called from the width of its leaves, because they are broad and wide. For *platus* is the Greek for flat, as I. (Thomas refers to Isidore) says. It has soft leaves similar to those of the vine, as the same says. Dio (-scorides) says that the maple is a cold and dry tree, whose leaves are valuable against feverish complaints. Therefore, decoctions of it are useful against burns and inflammed swellings of the eyes, and mixed with wine against poisons and other things that burn."[23]

Vincent's two chapters on the maple are also straightforward compilations, without any original contribution. But he drew much more on Pliny than his predecessors and by doing so introduced a certain limited amount of observed facts : " The plane tree has divided leaves and ample roots. As the cherry tree comes out with the early spring winds so does the plane tree. It is tough, and moist like the alder, but drier than elm and ash." [24]

But there is still a great difference between these few remarks, copied from Pliny, and Albert's description [25] : " Platanus is a very big tree, known in our country. In Germany and the Slav countries large buildings are made from these trees and very large tables. Therefore, there is no truth in the saying that they are small trees growing on the islands of Germany. For neither is Germany an island nor are there islands belonging to it, nor is the maple a small tree. On the contrary, it is of great bulk and as tall as big oak trees. It is a tree with ash-coloured bark, and when it has reached full size a very thick trunk. The tree goes high up before it starts spreading out into branches, and has roots of great depth. It thrives on soil gathered together by floods near the water, and on land a little moister than hilly country or on other high-lying country. It sinks its roots deep into such soil and has many of them. It has very white timber with spots whiter than the rest. It is these spots that make it such a handsome wood. Its leaf is in colour and shape like that of the vine, but smoother and thinner ; it is in size like that of the so-called *Vitis Sclava*. This tree has certain growths, sometimes in the roots, sometimes on the trunk, sometimes on the major branches, and these growths have transverse pores. (Albert apparently refers to bracket fungi, whose surface below is indeed covered with pores running at right angles to the horizontal growth of the fungus.) The maple has diverse ways of nutrition. Of it comes the noble myrrh, from which the most beautiful goblets and other utensils are made. The timber is suitable for buildings, especially for those which have subtly carved figures. Applied by doctors to the human body, it has the virtues of softening and moistening and maturing and mollifying. But it is not as important in medicine as in architecture."

Exactly the same literary development is to be found in the six descriptions of the oak tree. Of this, Isidore says only that its name (Quercus) derives from the fact that the gods here revealed the future to the asker (quaerentibus), that it is a very old tree, as proved by the tree Mambre, under which Abraham lived and which was supposed still to be thriving during the reign of the Emperor Constans. Its fruits, Isidore goes on, are called oak-galls. He distinguishes between two kinds, "ὀμφακίτης, which is small, hard, often knotty, and medicinally useful, and βάλανος, which is soft, light, less perforated, and (whose oil is) useful for lamps."

St. Hildegarde's text is again quite independent of Isidore's, but even less descriptive. She calls the oak cold, hard and bitter. "Its fruit is of no use to man for food, nor do even worms like to feed on its wood. When they try, they soon stop and leave it alone. Nevertheless, certain animals feed on the fruits and get fat on them, for instance pigs. Neither wood nor fruits are of use to medicine." That is all St. Hildegarde has to say.

Bartholomew the Englishman and Thomas of Cantimpré are again nearly identical, except that Thomas reduces Bartholomew's text to about half without adding a line of his own. "The oak," Bartholomew says, "is an acorn bearing tree, old, solid and compact, of hard bark and inside a softer pith or none. On its leaves it creates a certain astringent and tasteless sub-

59

stance which doctors call oak-gall. The oak carries fruits called acorns, on which pigs and also young boars are fattened. It has a strong and tortuous root which goes deep into the ground. Its bark, fruits and leaves are cold, astringent and dry and, therefore, medically useful.'' Then Bartholomew gives quotations from Isidore, Ovid and Jerome. He describes the acorns as round outside, oblong, very smooth, rather shiny ''and translucent like finger-nails.'' They grow, he says, between the leaves without any flowers appearing first. '' In the beginning they are green, but when reaching maturity they get a kind of tawny colour. They grow in small completely round little cups, smooth inside, but rough and somewhat hairy outside. . Inside they have a thick pith, divided by a sort of skin from the husk. Husk and pith are very dry and astringent''[26]. These remarks of Bartholomew show much more interest in the actual appearance of oak and acorn than those of any of his predecessors. They are followed by the usual medical advice.

Vincent also devotes a good deal of space to medical advice. His interest in observed facts goes about as far as Bartholomew's. But, instead of trusting his own eyes, he relies on the most detailed description available in antique literature : Pliny's *Natural History*. That he should do so will not seem surprising, if we remember that it was Vincent's age which rediscovered the genuine qualities of Greek and Roman science and art. Thus, Vincent quotes the following passages from various books of Pliny, but chiefly the sixteenth : ''The common oak produces acorns just like the holm-oak, the hard oak and the cork-oak. The acorns of the common oak make a pig very corpulent and heavy. They are the sweetest of all acorns. The timber of the oak is the strongest, the least liable to decay, and the most suitable for dressing hides. It is rich in branches, but none the less very high and thick in the trunk. The common oak produces the most highly praised fungi, the hard oak and the cyprus tree the most harmful ones. The common oak comes down to level ground, like the maple, the dogwood and the ash." [27]

Vincent and Bartholomew are separated from Albert by no more than fifteen or twenty years. Yet the difference between their remarks on the oak and his is decisive. Albert seems to have used Bartholomew and certainly knew Pliny and Dioscorides. But his chief intention is—and in this he appears as great an innovator as the sculptors of Rheims—to describe precisely what he had seen and investigated himself. There was at his time no botanical vocabulary in existence which he could have used. He had to create his own terminology, just as the carvers had to develop their own idiom. They were more successful. Their results are convincing to this day. Albert's strike us as awkward and somewhat turgid. But the meaning of his roundabout descriptions is sound all the same, and the effort to convey it in a medium never before in the West used for such purposes adds originality and freshness.

This is what Albert says : " The oak is a very big, tall and wide-branched tree with many big and deep roots and a bark, rough when it gets older, but soft in its youth. It possesses very big branches. The leaf is thick, broad and hard, when it has reached full strength, and can be entirely circumscribed by triangles with their bases on the leaf (he means : along the axis of the leaf) and their apexes outside. The leaf keeps to the tree for a long time, even when it is dry. The wood grows out of upright layers with upright pores (he means : it is straight-grained), can easily be cut perpendicularly, is easily hewable, and suitable for figure-

carving. For this purpose, however, boxwood is better
still. The outside layers of the timber are white,
towards the inside they merge into red. In water it
first floats, but later sinks, because of its terrestriality
(an Aristotelian conception), and gets black. . . . Its
fruit is called the acorn. It is not attached to the twig
on which it grows by its own little bract, but little cups
develop on the twig, and in these the acorns sprout
forth. The acorn has outside a hard pod which holds
it. It is like wood, very smooth and of a columnar
shape, except that it is not flat at the top, but ends
hemispherically with a point in the middle like the
mark of the pole. At the bottom it has its base with
which it sucks nourishment out of its cup. This base
also has not a completely plain surface, but is a kind
of hemisphere considerably flattened at the pole. It is
in contact with the place of nourishment, but not
merely in a point. Otherwise it could not draw sufficient nourishment. (Albert apparently means that the
whole bottom of the acorn must touch the cup and not
only a pole-like point in order to establish enough contact between the two for the sucking up of food). The
acorn in its pod has a skin which is not hard but soft.
This develops out of the husk of the acorn, and the acorn
is wrapped up in it and has a division along the middle,
as though a column had its surface cut throughout its
length. On the top it has the seed, and what appears
of a mealy substance below is purified into food for the
seed. The cup in which the acorn itself sits is concave,
well formed, almost as if it were turned. Its bottom
is somewhat flat, and sitting in this the acorn draws its
food. The outside of the cup is scaly and rough because
of its terrestriality, which has been purified from the substance of the acorn (?). It is not connected with the
twig either by a little bract or a hanging stalk. Instead

of that it sits immediately on the twig. The reason of this is that the acorn should not be too far away from the twig, because if the acorn had to suck its nourishment up a long distance this would get hard and cold on the way and be of no use, especially since the juice of the oak is very terrestrial. On the leaves of the oak you can often find a round growth like a ball which is called the oak-gall. If this has been there for some time it brings forth a maggot." This last sentence shows Albert aware of the growth of the gall insect within the twig. Whether he realized that this was the natural result of the development of an egg deposited within the twig, or whether he regarded it as a case of spontaneous generation, in which Antiquity and the Middle Ages firmly believed, must remain doubtful. Albert's description is followed by prognostications from the oak-gall for cold or mild winters, and by a paragraph of medical superstition[28].

Be they as they may, Albert's powers of seeing and describing remain a convincing parallel to those of the Rheims and Southwell masters. He wrote about 1250-1275, the Rheims capitals must be of about 1250-1260, those of Southwell, we know, belong to the last years of the thirteenth century.

This historical parallel does not, of course, mean that the master masons read Albert the Great. They certainly did not, although the bishops and abbots for whom they worked did. Yet even so, it can hardly be assumed that these would influence—not the sculptor's programme, but the sculptor's manner to such an extent and in such a direction.

So we are left with the only explanation which historical experience justifies ; the existence of a spirit of the age, operating in art as well as philosophy, in religion as well as politics. This spirit works changes in style and outlook, and the man of genius is not he who tries to shake off its bonds, but he to whom it is given to express it in the most powerful form. And what else can at any time enforce expression but the spirit of the age ? Eternal problems : love, truth, duty—yes, but in terms of changing ages and styles, different in Dante's worship of Beatrice, in the personal yet polished passion of Shakespeare's Sonnets, and again in Goethe's so much more intimate and indiscreet lyrics.

But once it is admitted that the leaves of Southwell are what they are, because of a specific spirit of their age, must we not go farther and ask ourselves, whether the tracing of parallels with a literature of scientific observation is really sufficient to explain their moving intensity ? Surely, a spirit of exact description alone would not have made them so noble. What, then, is there beyond the new scientific curiosity and awareness to nature in Western thought and emotion of the thirteenth century that would help to explain the greatness, the fullness and the poise of the Southwell capitals ?

Two mottoes have been placed above the beginning of this little book. To one we have referred before. It is from the song of a wandering scholar, lighthearted and in love with the woods, the flowers, and his girl. The other has the same keen delight in nature, but a delight deepened by the naïve faith of one of the most lovable of Christian saints. If St. Francis greets the sun as his brother and the earth '' that bringeth forth fruit and bright flowers and herbs '' as his mother, he feels that what makes their beauty and what makes him see their beauty is that they and he and everything are the Lord's creation, God's children.

St. Francis was the first, it seems, to feel this oneness of the universe. St. Thomas Aquinas brought it into the most comprehensive philosophic system of the Middle Ages. His theory of beauty encompasses the beauty of the things of this world, instead of denying it, as the centuries before him had done. His more popular contemporary Vincent of Beauvais professed in a famous passage : "I am moved with spiritual sweetness towards the creator and ruler of this world when I behold the magnitude and beauty and permanence of his creation."[29]

To show the fundamental contrast between this attitude and the harsh dualism of a hundred years earlier two examples may be given. Of the great St. Bernard of Clairvaux his biographer says that after a year as a novice in a monastery he did not know yet whether the hall in which he lived had a vaulted or a flat ceiling and believed that the church in which he prayed had one window in the apse, whereas it had three. "So much," the *Vita* continues, "was he absorbed in spiritual things, so completely was his hope directed towards God, so much his mind occupied with meditation that he saw and yet did not see, that he heard and yet did not hear (videns non videbat, audiens non audiebat)."[30]

And St. Anselm, Archbishop of Canterbury, one of the earliest scholastic philosophers, who died about 1125, writes of flowers on only one occasion. But far from describing or appreciating them, he introduces them only to illustrate the tenet that "the delight of the senses is rarely good, mostly bad." He divides the evils of the senses in a typically scholastic way into categories according to how many senses are active. So we are told that sight and smell are accomplices in the evil of admiring red roses, and sight, hearing and smell, "when someone sits in a garden to look at the herbs, listen to stories and breathe the scent of the flowers.''[31]

Such a description of the worldly sinner seems written to warn the poet and the romancing knight. This cannot be the case, since St. Anselm lived nearly a hundred years before the great days of troubadour poetry. However, even the chivalrous romance of the thirteenth century is not wholly worldly when treated by one who in genius and originality might be compared to St. Francis. Thus, the theme of Wolfram of Eschenbach's *Parzival*, the greatest of mediæval epics (about 1215) is the education of the Christian Knight from sheer courage to charity and *maasze,* the *mezura* of the Provençal poets, that is, right measure—or what in the case of Southwell has been described as balance. And this ideal of balance is in one place defined by Wolfram as keeping one's soul pledged to God without losing hold of the world. It is the ideal of St. Louis, King of France, whose ''granz chivalries '' against the infidels in the Crusade of 1250 and whose humility before the monks of France are described by Joinville. It is also St. Thomas's ideal of beauty : Consonance out of diverging elements—a surprisingly Sophoclean ideal.

And is not the balance of Southwell something deeper too than a balance of nature and style or of the imitative and the decorative ? Is it not perhaps also a balance of God and World, the invisible and the visible ? Could these leaves of the English countryside, with all their freshness, move us so deeply if they were not carved in that spirit which filled the saints and poets and thinkers of the thirteenth century, the spirit of religious respect for the loveliness of created nature ? The inexhaustible delight in live form that can be touched with worshipping fingers and felt with all senses is ennobled—consciously in the philosophy of

66

Thomas, the science of Albert, and the romance of Wolfram, unconsciously in the carving of the butter-cups and thorn leaves and maple leaves of Southwell—by the conviction that so much beauty can exist only because God is in every man and beast, in every herb and stone. The Renaissance in the South two hundred years later was perhaps once again capable of such worship of beauty, but no firm faith was left to strengthen it.

Seen in this light, the leaves of Southwell assume a new significance as one of the purest symbols surviving in Britain of Western thought, our thought, in its loftiest mood.

NOTES

(1) The translation of the *Cantico del Sole* is that of the Swan Press, Chelsea, 1927. The original lines are as follows :

Laudato sii, mio Signore, con tutte le tue creature,
specialmente messer lo frate sole,
lo quale giorna, e allumini per lui.
Ed ello è bello e radiante con grande splendore ;
da te, altissimo, porta significazione.

Laudato sii, mio Signore, per sora luna e le stelle,
in cielo l'hai formato chiarite e preziose e belle.

Laudato sii, mio Signore, per frate vento
e per aere e nuvolo e sereno e ogni tempo
per i quali alle tue creature dai sustentamento.

Laudato sii, mio Signore, per sora acqua,
la quale è molto utile e umida e preziosa e costa.

Laudato sii, mio Signore, per frate foco,
per lo quale ennallumi nila notte,
ed ello è bello e giocando e robustoso e forte.

Laudato sii, mio Signore, per sora nostra madre terra,
la quale ne sustenta e governa
e produce diversi frutti, con coloriti fiori ed erba.

(2) The poem is No. 103 of the Schmoller edition. In translation, it means : The grove puts on its clothes of leaves. The nightingale begins to sing. The fields are getting lovely with many colours. Now it is delightful to go for walks through the woods. More delightful is it to pick lilies and roses. But the greatest delight of all is to play with a pretty girl.

(3) See A. F. Leach : *Visitations and Memorials of Southwell Minster*, Camden Society, 1891, p. 211. On the building history of Southwell Minster in general, see A. Hamilton Thompson in *Transactions of the Thoroton Society*, Nottingham, vol. XV, 1911, and *Memorials of Old Nottinghamshire*, 1912. A document of 1292 quoted in the literature on Southwell appears in the original text (see *Calendars of Inquisitions Miscellaneous preserved at the Public Record Office*, vol. I, 1916, No. 1587) not to have any provable connection with the chapter house.

(4) See E. S. Prior : *A History of Gothic Art in England*, 1900, p. 319.

(5) *Proceedings of the Cambridge Antiquarian Society*, vol. XXXV, 1935, pp. 1-32.

(6) Professor Salisbury drew my attention to the surprising skill displayed in rendering the difference between *Quercus pedunculata* on the capital and *Quercus sessiliflora* (*petrea*) in the spray at the springing of the arches.

(7) Professor Salisbury was especially taken with the exact interpretation in stone of the hairy surface of the smallest leaves in the centre. He is convinced that the plant portrayed is hemp nettle and not mint as Professor Seward suggested. Hedge woundwort is another but much less likely possibility according to Professor Salisbury.

(8) For the history of gardening in the Middle Ages, see Sir Frank Crisp : *Mediaeval Gardens,* 1924, and M. L. Gothein : *A History of Garden Art,* 1928.

(9) See G. Dehio, 1924 ; W. Noack, 1925 ; W. Pinder and W. Hege, 1927.

(10) See H. R. Hahnloser, Vienna, 1935 ; R. Darcel and J. B. A. Lassus, Paris, 1856 (English edition by R. Willis, 1859).

(11) See H. Kunze : *Das Fassadenproblem der französischen Früh- und Hochgotik,* Thesis, Strassburg, 1909, published, 1912. Also : Anthyme Saint Paul. *Bulletin Monumental,* vol. LXX, 1906, and E. Panofsky, *Jahrbuch für Kunstwissenschaft,* 1927. The facts are that the old cathedral was consumed by fire in 1210, that re-building started in 1211 and the new choir was consecrated in 1241. On the floor of the nave was, down to the eighteenth century, a labyrinth pattern into whose corners the names of the first chief master masons were inscribed, with their principal work and, in the case of three, their duration of office. They were Jean d'Orbais, the first (according to Professor Panofsky the second), who began the chancel (Panofsky : vaulted the chancel)—no length of appointment mentioned—then Jean Le Loup, " who began the portals " (16 years), Gaucher de Reims, " who worked on the portals and *voussures* " (voussoirs or, according to Panofsky, nave vaults ; 8 years), and Bernard de Soissons, " who completed five vaults (probably of the nave) and the rose window " (35 years). An existing document about Bernard is dated 1287. If he died immediately after that year, he would have been appointed in 1253, Gaucher in 1245, Le Loup in 1229. Thus, the west portals cannot have been started before 1229. The nave was probably not put in hand before the choir was ready, that is c. 1240. The triforium gallery is fairly high up and may well be part of Bernard's wo͏̷ that is later than 1253. Similar foliage and figures follow

69

their style immediately that of the most advanced figures of the west façade appear inside the west front up to and around the rose window. They may date from 1260 or 1270. On French Gothic foliage, see Lambin : *La Flore Gothique*, 1893, and *La Flore des grandes cathédrales de France*, 1897 (two books which, owing to the war, I have not been able to use), and D. Jalabert, *Bulletin Monumental*, vol. XCI, 1932, where a capital from the Ste. Chapelle is illustrated. More French examples in Joan Evans : *Nature in Design*, 1933. I know of no list of plants occurring at Reims. The species given by Dr. Evans for Chartres, and by Mlle. Jalabert for the Ste. Chapelle, however, are strikingly similar to the Southwell list. Ste. Chapelle : oak, hawthorn, maple, ivy, hop, buttercup, and fig, holly, hepatica and artemisia.

(12) On the York Chapter House windows, see J. Browne : *A description of the Representations in the Windows of York Minster*, etc., 1859.

(13) M. Raynouard : *Choix des Poésies Originales des Troubadours*, vol. 3, 1818, p. 53 ; J. Anglade : *Anthologie des Troubadours*, 1927, p. 42 ; A. Berry : *Florilège des Troubadours*, 1930, p. 164. The latter two editions have prose translations into modern French. On the philological problem of the poem, see V. Crescini ; *Romanica Fragmenta*, 1932.

(14) On the history of mediæval thought, see H. Osborn Taylor: *The Mediæval Mind*, 3rd edition, 1919. On the history of mediæval science : Lynn Thorndike : *A History of Magic and Experimental Science*, volumes 1 and 2, 1923, and G. Sarton : *Introduction to the History of Science*, vol. 2, Carnegie Institution of Washington, 1931. Also C. Homer Haskins : *Studies in the History of Mediæval Science*, 1924. On mediæval botany the most recent book is H. Fischer : *Mittelalterliche Pflanzenkunde*, Munich, 1929. On the mediæval attitude to nature and the degree to which nature, scenery and flowers could be enjoyed by mediæval poets, writers and philosophers W. Ganzenmüller : *Das Naturgefühl im Mittelalter*, 1914, and A. Biese : *Die Entwicklung des Naturgefühls im Mittelalter und in der Neuzeit*, 1892.

(15) *De Causis et Proprietatibus Elementorum et Planetarum*, part I, tract 2, chap. 9, ed. Borgnet.

(16) On Albert's position in the history of botany, see E. H. F. Meyer : *Geschichte der Botanik*, vol. 4, 1857; A. Fellner : *Albertus*

Magnus als Botaniker, 1881, and J. Wimmer : *Deutsches Pflanzen-leben nach Albertus Magnus,* 1908.

(17) *Studies in the History and Methods of Science,* vol. 2, 1921.

(18) Book 17, chap. 7, sec. 37. See Migne : *Patrologia Latina,* vol. 82.

(19) It stands in the *Liber Subtilitatum* which Professor Singer regards as spurious (*Studies in the History and Methods of Science,* vol. 1, 1917); but Lynn Thorndike and G. Sarton have—successfully, as far as I can see—re-stated St. Hildegarde's claim to the treatise.

(20) Migne : *Patrologia Latina,* vol. 197 : book 1, chap. 30.

(21) The verse is Ecclesiasticus 24, 19. Isidore quotes it in a different form (see above in the text).

(22) Book 17, chap. 119. I am quoting from the printed edition of 1483.

(23) I am quoting from the manuscript; Lincoln College 57, kindly placed at my disposal by the late Rector of the College, Mr. J. A. R. Munro. The description of the plane tree is fol. 65 r.

(24) I am quoting from the printed Venetian edition of 1591. *Speculum Naturale,* book 12, chap. 187.

(25) Ed. Brognet, vol. 10, 1891, p. 199 (Book 6, tract 1, chap. 30).

(26) Oak : Isidore : book 17, chap. 7, sec. 38 ; Hildegarde : book 1, chap. 25 ; Bartholomew : book 17, chap. 134 ; Thomas : fol. 65 v.

(27) Book 12, chap. 191.

(28) Book 6, tract 1, chap. 31, p. 203 (Borgnet).

(29) On St. Thomas's aesthetics, see M. de Wulf : Les Théories esthétiques propres à St. Thomas, *Revue Néo-Scholastique* vol. 3, No. 2, p. 133 seq. ; P. Vallet : *L'Idée du Beau dans la philosophie de St. Thomas d'Aquin,* 1883. Also M. Dvořák : *Idealismus und Natural-ismus in der gotischen Skulptur und Malerei, Historische Zeitschrift,* vol. 119, 1918 (reprinted in *Kunstgeschichte als Geistesgeschichte,* 1924), where quotations from St. Thomas are placed side by side with passages from Vincent of Beauvais. In addition, compare : Taylor's *Mediæval Mind,* quoted above, note 14 ; and E. Rosenthal: *Giotto,* 1924.

(30) Migne : *Patrologia Latina,* vol. 185, p. 238.

(31) Migne : *Patrologia Latina,* vol. 159, pp. 609-610.

ACKNOWLEDGMENTS

The author wishes to express his gratitude to Professor E. J. Salisbury for botanical, Professor E. H. Warmington for philological, and John Rodker for literary help and advice. Some of the illustrations in the text are not from photographs by Mr. Attenborough. This refers to figures 10 to 21 and 23 to 24. Figures 17 to 20 are reproduced by kind permission of the National Buildings Record, figures 23 and 24 by the courtesy of Mr. F. H. Crossley, figure 21 by permission of Messrs. Walter Scott. The plan on page 19 is redrawn from volume XXXV of the proceedings of the Cambridge Antiquarian Society.

Plate 1 *In the ante-room of the Chapter House*

Plate 2   *Left side of archway into the Chapter House*

Plate 3   *Right side of archway into the Chapter House*

Oak capitals in the ante-room (V.4)

Plate 4

Plate 5

Hawthorn capitals in the ante-room (V · 5)

Plate 6   Vine (Mulberry ? Capital

Plate 7   *Vine (Mulberry ? C.36)*

Plate 8

Plate 9   *Vine* (C.20)

Plate 10   Oak (Capital a)

Plate 11   *Oak (C.12)*

Plate 12   *Maple (Capital e)*

Plate 13   Maple (C.39)

Plate 14   Maple (C.19)

Plate 15

Maple (C. 5)

Plate 16   Buttercup (Capital c)

Plate 17

Buttercup (C. 13)

Plate 18   Buttercup (Centre shaft of archway

Plate 19   *Buttercup (Capital d)*

Plate 20

Buttercup (C. 4)

Plate 21

Hop (C. 34)

Plate 22

Plate 23

Hop (C.14)

Plate 24   Bryony (C. 15)

Plate 25   Bryony (C. 42)

Plate 26   *Ivy—Hare and Hounds* (C. 24)

Ivy—Hare and Hounds (C.24)

Plate 28   Hawthorn (C. 3

Plate 29

Hawthorn and Hemp Nettle (C.22)

Plate 30   Hawthorn (Capital f)

Plate 31   *Hawthorn (Buttercup ? Outer archway)*

Plate 32   Rose (C.9)